Seydou's Christmas Tree

Seydou's Christmas Tree

BY

Joel Thurtell

Hardalee Press

Published by Hardalee Press

11803 Priscilla Lane

Plymouth, MI 48170

Library of Congress Control Number: 2009906577

Thurtell, Joel Howard

ISBN 978-0-9759969-1-1

Cover and interior design by Maya Rhodes

Tree graphic © Vasilkin / Dreamstime.com

Seydou's Christmas Tree

Phil — But for Karen,
I would never have
served in the Peace
corps. It was a
shared experience
that shaped both of
us.

Joel Martin
6-24-2015

I think of Seydou's Christmas tree every year in the final countdown to December 25. It was the extraordinary gift of a Muslim boy to his two Christian friends.

I learned a profound lesson from a young African boy, yet it seems every year I have to re-learn from the experience. Each year, it comes down to this: We wait until Christmas is nearly past before deciding it's high time we had a tree. Then we head for the Michigan hills where they grow evergreen trees to be cut for Christmas.

For years, we had this ritual where my wife, our two sons and I would tromp through the snow, straightening trees, shaking off snow and ice, standing back

to gauge their bare spots, looking for the perfect Christmas tree. Each of us had a different opinion about just what made the best Christmas tree, so it always took some time for us to settle on one that was just right.

One time, I noticed that many of these supposedly all-natural trees had a uniformly dark cast to them. Looking closer, I could see why. The blue-green wasn't confined just to the needles, but had been painted onto twigs, branches and trunks. The trees had been spray-painted!

I stared at the dark patina of paint and declared, "This is NOT a Christmas tree!"

The statement, once out of my mouth, had a familiar sound to it. Where had I heard—no, where had I *said* that before?

It was once upon a time, many years ago in a country far, far from the chill evergreen farms and Christmas-tree sales lots of Michigan.

My wife and I were Peace Corps volunteers in Togo, a tiny West African country. Togo is a sliver of land stretching from the balmy Atlantic to the incredibly hot, dry, windy savannas that lead to the Sahara.

Karen and I were living in the big market town of Dapaong, in the far north of Togo. She was teaching health education in public schools and hospitals. I was building a three-room school in the distant village of Nano. I was also finishing a school in another town, Djangou, where the previous American volunteer had gotten hepatitis and had to go home.

There was no water supply in Djangou, so I took it upon myself to have a well dug there. Most days, I would drive my little Yamaha 80 motorcycle out to one of the towns to work on the schools or see how the well was going. It was a hot, dusty trip. To start toward Nano, you took the International Highway, called that because it started on the Atlantic at Togo's

capital, Lomé, and ran north through Dapaong and on to Upper Volta (now called Burkina Faso) and then into the Sahara. In those days, this highway was little more than a single lane dirt washboard. But Nano wasn't on the highway. I had to navigate a goat track most of the way. That was okay in dry times, but when it rained, it was very slippery and look out!

That little path led past amazing sights. Even after many months of living in northern Togo, there were times when I wanted to pinch myself, because the landscape with its towering baobabs and flat-silhou-etted nere trees, the circular, mud household walls and round, orange clay houses with conical thatched roofs seemed incredibly alien to my Midwestern eyes.

After work, which involved mixing mortar, mak-ing bricks, raising pillars, building roof trusses, setting a rock foundation and laying a concrete floor in tem-peratures well over 100 degrees, I would jump on my motorcycle and head home to Dapaong. We lived in a

mud house with tar-covered walls and a corrugated-metal roof. There was no running water or electricity. We were Americans, so we would light kerosene lanterns to be able to read at night. Most of our neighbors just went to bed when the sun went down.

Outside, we had a small walled latrine, with metal roof, divided into two parts—one for showers and one for the other stuff. Behind our house was a low, roofless clay platform with a knee-high adobe wall around it. The adobe was painted with tar. This platform was the mosque. At five in the morning, a man known as a *muezzin* would call the neighborhood men to prayers with a musical chant. It was a haunting sound, and to this day I can still hear, still sing the tune.

Near the open-air mosque was a wide hole in the ground where people dropped buckets on ropes to pull up muddy water. That was where our water came from, mostly, and it was mainly a boy named Seydou who got it for us.

Seydou Bukari was about thirteen. He lived in a sprawling adobe house right behind us. His dad was the *imam*, the man who led prayers. He was called "El Hadji" because he'd been to Mecca. Seydou's mom was Assana, a remarkable woman who could speak many languages, even a few words of English she'd learned from us Peace Corps types. Assana adopted the Americans and made sure we had what we needed to survive.

Seydou was an amazingly adaptable, inventive kid who was flunking out of the rigid, French-style Togolese elementary school he attended. In all matters that fell outside the classroom, Seydou was an expert.

At the height of the dry season, for example, when there had been no rain for months and most of the private wells were dry, local authorities occasionally, without announcement, allowed families in our neighborhood to fill buckets with water from municipal pumps. We Americans never knew when this

would happen. The faucets were never open long, because the city wells were nearly dry, too. So, if you missed it, you were out of luck—this was the best water for cooking, bathing, drinking, because it came from a deep well and was not full of clay.

Somehow, Seydou always found out when the pumps were open. He'd come bounding up to our door, rubbing his hand over his head and face slowly in his unique mannerism of pubescent self-consciousness, and proclaim that if we gave him our buckets, he'd get them filled.

Seydou was a mechanical wizard in a country so poor in everything, including spare parts for machines, that it paid to know how to improvise. The word you would hear Togolese utter following the resurrection of some apparently dead mechanism was "*se débrouiller*," meaning to get oneself cleverly out of a jam. Seydou was a top-notch *débrouillard*. Using cast-off parts, he had assembled a bicycle. Most To-

golese kids didn't have bikes, so this was a real feat.

But Seydou's bike turned out to be rather small, and its wheel rims didn't fit standard-size tires and inner tubes. For Seydou, that was a problem that could be dealt with. He would sit for hours outside our house patiently cutting sections out of tires and inner tubes and gluing the ends together. When the glue was firm, he'd pump up his tires and get a day or two of hard riding in before the seal began to leak. Then he'd redo the whole process.

We had tremendous faith in Seydou's ingenuity. He was the fastest chicken-dresser I ever saw. We bought our chickens and guinea fowl live and hired Seydou to kill and clean them. He was adept at starting a charcoal fire without the help of kerosene. Amazingly, he'd invented a sort of "stereo" system. He hung a small loudspeaker from his radio by its wires inside a teapot, making what I'd have to call—well—not a boom box, but maybe a boom kettle.

Only one project bombed and that was when he had the notion of stocking his mother's well with catfish. It was all right until one of the fish died.

It seemed Seydou could fix anything. He was never afraid to speak to us Americans of his ideas, always rubbing that hand self-consciously over his head and downward across his brow. It was in that manner that Seydou one day shortly before Christmas broached the subject he called "*arbre de Noël.*"

If we wanted a Christmas tree, Seydou said, he knew where there were lots of them.

It took me a minute to catch on to what he meant. Northern Togo is about as close to desert as you can get without being really a desert. It's broken up here and there by a few mountains that resemble mesas, but its mostly rolling hills are low, and in December the wind wails down from the real desert—a hard, penetrating, cold wind that carries orange dust so thick it turns the equatorial sun into a dimly glowing

orb. Harmattan is also the time for burning, even in town, where I was told scorching the land made it easier to spot the cobras and pit vipers whose bite can kill you within minutes So, with the hard-flung dust of harmattan we had the human-created smoke from grass fires. The blasting dust, the blazing fires and the suffocating smoke gave us a profound sense of everlasting heat. Those chill, evergreen-decked hills of Michigan seemed so remote they might as well not have existed.

Christmas trees?

It's hard for anything to grow in northern Togo. Least of all pine trees.

Seydou definitely was talking Christmas trees, though. I guessed he'd seen something in the market, maybe little plastic evergreens.

No, Seydou replied. Not fake trees. Alive and growing.

Christmas trees? I wondered. Thriving in the blis-

tering semidesert of northern Togo?

It occurred to me that something may have been missing in translation. Seydou was not a Christian. There was nothing in his background to give him either the knowledge of or feeling for the Christian celebration of Jesus' birth. Seydou was of the Mossi people, originally a warrior tribe from Upper Volta. While he, too, worshiped one God, he did so through the Prophet Muhammad, not Jesus Christ. No way could Seydou understand our concept of an evergreen tree decorated with lights, tinsel, popcorn and stars and signifying birth and everlasting life.

Yet here was this young Muslim boy asserting that there not only were *"arbres de Noël"* in Togo, but that he, Seydou Bukari, would lead us directly to them.

How did Seydou know about Christmas trees? He claimed to have supplied a tree to Peace Corps people who preceded us. But as honest as I knew Seydou to be, I could not believe in an evergreen tree—a Christmas tree—in this hothouse, Togo. My God, we were living on the last step before the Sahara! Remember, Seydou, I said, This is December, harmattan, the time of the dry wind. The temperature never falls below the 90s when the sun is out, and mostly it stays well over 100. We haven't seen a cloud in four months. Look, I said, you can actually see the wind, see it laden heavy with the very Sahara, that load of orange grit that makes everything a haze and covers newly washed clothes with dust before they can dry.

No, he said, this was a true thing. He was talking about Christmas trees, nothing else.

The idea took root.

Combined with my implicit trust in Seydou, the basic unreality of my surroundings opened me to that irrational thing called faith. We were so far from home, so far from our family and old friends. This country was so strange it felt unreal. Riding my Yamaha along the international highway, I would come upon an el-

ephant casually munching leaves from a tree. A troop of baboons might run alongside my path for a ways, or I might halt so a scimitar-toothed creature big as a freezer chest could plod off the road. This was a wart-hog. Hiking to the Dapaong market, I would pass the soccer field, where two sets of barefoot players were raising dust while spectators used trees as bleachers.

When our well at Djangou came in a gusher, word got out that the American could work magic. I had dowsed that well, using a forked mango stick that truly did bend at times, though I eventually placed the well where I wanted it to go—near the school where it would serve the whole village. People would ask me to "witch" wells, but first I had to be inter-viewed by the village *fetisheur*, the witch doctor with his collection of feathers, bones, bottle caps and in-cantations.

The cries of the *muezzin*, the ululating wails at funerals, the cackling of guinea fowl, the ground-

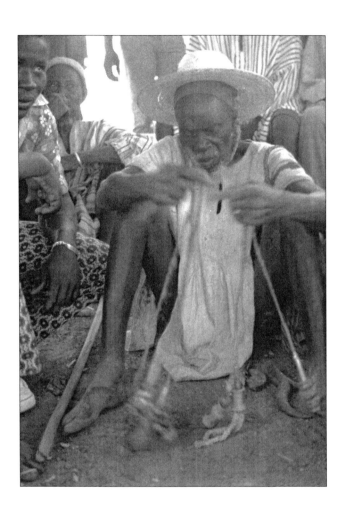

thumping roar of trucks with bad mufflers or none at all and the staccato clatter of rattles strapped to dancers' legs—these were just a few of the sights and sounds that helped me know I was a long way from home.

As I bounced along the trail far from any village or even a farmer's compound, I'd pass fields where people had strewn broken clay pots. These were graveyards, I was told, and the broken pots symbolized both loss and release. How unlike the uniform rows of marble and granite cenotaphs in an American cemetery. There were no names on these pots, as if the Afterlife would regard earthly monickers of no use.

There were times when I'd stand on our stoop at night and watch people's shadows flicker across our yard, thrown there by a cook-fire in a nearby compound. You could barely make out the curvature of the mud-walled compound and the cone top hat of the thatched roof. Voices spoke rapidly in some lan-

guage that was completely incomprehensible—Mossi or Ghourma, Moba or maybe Hausa. I felt as if I'd stumbled into a living diorama at some museum of anthropology.

As far away as Michigan and our families were, the thought of Christmas seemed to pull us closer. I wanted to find a Christmas tree, even if this was Togo, where my wish was an impossibility. So one day, a week or so before Christmas, we asked Seydou to show us his famous evergreens.

Karen and I hopped on our motorcycles. Seydou sat behind me, holding a saw and a ball of twine to tie the tree to one of our bikes. It was a little after noon, and it was terribly hot. We'd gone a few kilometers, and of course there were no trees. I was thinking how the excursion was a waste when Seydou shouted, "C'est ici!"

Well, here we are, I thought doubtfully. We stopped. I looked around. What a bust.

Flat land. No grass. The ground was hard clay. No trees, no shade, only some scrub brush covered with orange dust.

"So where are these Christmas trees?" we asked.

"There's one!" Seydou pointed.

I looked again. Nothing.

"There's another! All around here!" Seydou said excitedly.

He was running now, looking at each of the bushes. Finally he stood beside one. I couldn't believe it. Seydou thought these ragamuffin scavenger plants were Christmas trees!

"These are NOT Christmas trees!" I said.

I parked my motorcycle. We walked to the bush where Seydou stood smiling, rubbing his forehead in self-conscious pleasure. I looked at the bush. It was the scraggliest, ugliest piece of vegetation I'd ever seen. No leaves. No needles.

"Christmas trees!" Seydou said. He who had never

seen a real Christmas tree was delighted to show us a whole plain full of them.

I looked again at the trees. Well, they were NOT trees. They were at best bushes. And there was no way to disguise their nasty, misshapen form. It was a species meant only for the sub-Sahara. Nevertheless, I had to admit that they did have needles, after all. Flat, sharp needles. Not pine needles. More like cactus needles.

We circled a bush, looking it over again and again. Soon, our circles were wider, as we looked at others. Unconsciously, we were doing what we did on the parking lot Christmas tree emporiums of the United States—searching for the perfect Christmas tree.

Okay, they were not trees. But they WERE bushes. However, those needles couldn't be mistaken for anything but thorns.

Thornbushes.

But here we were, sizing up these hideous excuses

for pine trees, discussing, seriously discussing, which would make the best ornamental tree.

Why not? What, after all, is a Christmas tree? It's not mentioned in the New Testament. Like the celebration of Christmas itself, it is a European invention of the Middle Ages. So, if Jesus had thought of using a tree, say as the nub of one of his parables, might He not have chosen such a nondescript, contemptible bush? Not a beautiful tree, symbolizing the pride of owning something perfect, but a poor, raggedy stick scrabbling humbly for its very existence and somehow surviving even on the verge of desert.

Seydou patiently explained how we could take it back. Easy. Just rope it to my Yamaha and carry it back with Seydou sitting triumphantly atop the Christmas tree.

Sounded like a plan. I walked back to my motorcycle and got the saw.

Seydou was grinning broadly. He knew just what

we'd do—drape strings of popcorn and paper snow-flakes over the tree as he'd seen our predecessors do.

Seydou was right. There ARE Christmas trees in Africa.

Photo Captions

page 2: Michigan Christmas trees

page 5: Togolese market

page 6: School at Nano

page 7: Well-digging

page 8: Seydou washing motorcycles

page 10: Baobab trees

page 12: Our house in Dapaong

page 14: Neighborhood well in Dapaong

page 15: Assana

page 17: Seydou

page 19: Seydou riding his bike

page 21: Seydou, me, Karen, Assana, her daughter

      Fati, a neighbor

Photographs by the author except page 21

About the Author

Joel Thurtell was a Peace Corps volunteer building schools and wells in northern Togo, West Africa in the early 1970s. He was editor of the Berrien Springs *Journal Era*, reporter for the *South Bend Tribune* and *Detroit Free Press* and has written for *The New York Times, The Progressive, The National Fisherman, QST, CQ, Electric Radio* and he writes a blog, joelontheroad. com.

He is co-author of *Up the Rouge! Paddling Detroit's Hidden River*, an environmental book published by Wayne State University Press; *Plug Nickel*, a collection of his essays on sailing and restoring wooden sailboats; *Shoestring Reporter: How I Got to be a Big City Reporter (Without Going to J School) and How You Can Do it Too!*, a primer on how to self-start a writing career, and the forthcoming *Mouse Code*, a book for young people of all ages about how field mice invented radio.

Trained as a historian at Kalamazoo College and the University of Michigan, he has been a congressional aide, printer's helper, grapevine trimmer, rural letter carrier, blueberry picker, foundry grinder, taxicab driver, repairer of rare books and restorer and re-seller of old ham radios.

He is currently writing and preparing books for publication and lives with his wife, Karen Fonde, M.D., and their lapdog Patti, in Plymouth, Michigan.

LaVergne, TN USA
21 August 2009
155532LV00002B/1/P